The Blue Absolute

T0160014

BOOKS & CHAPBOOKS BY AARON SHURIN

Flowers & Sky: Two Talks
The Skin of Meaning: Collected Literary Essays and Talks
Citizen
King of Shadows
Threshold (with Helen Douglas)
Involuntary Lyrics
Three Scenes from the Sauna at the YMCA
A Door
The Paradise of Forms: Selected Poems
Unbound: A Book of AIDS
Codex
Four Views Out of Paris
Into Distances
Narrativity
A's Dream
Elsewhere
The Graces
Giving up the Ghost
Toot Suite
The Night Sun
Woman on Fire

The Blue Absolute
Aaron Shurin

Nightboat Books
New York

ISBN: 978-1-64362-016-9

Typeset in: LTC Garamont
Graphic design: Brian Hochberger

Cataloging-in-publication data is available from the Library of Congress

Nightboat Books
New York
www.nightboat.org

Contents

I. SKIN OF CLOUDS

II. TO MAKE THE AIR THERE

III. THE INSCRUTABLE EDGE OF FLIGHT

I.   *Skin of Clouds*

THE EMISSARY

All the sky in that window . . . opens . . . where he can chase
the gulls into that white-diffused blue . . . and slurp the pinkish
clouds . . . then does he look back? Does he remember? Does
he travel freely in a circuit — horizon to home — spinning
in wild space but anchored to his walnut desk, his purple
shoes, his marble pen? Let it go he moans let them go! Could
he un-blot the page to keep his options wet, steer for the
hills, bank into updrafts over the Sea of Cortez, rise with
the wind, harness the air, ride the currents, not look back?
I watch him flirt with distances, open my shirt to the skin
so he can breathe me in and calculate the distance home . . .
There's a pot of mushroom soup on the stove . . . bread thick
as a bed and moist with molasses . . . I see him swerve, soaring
back, speeding like a comet, his hair slicked down, crackling
crystals on his face. His eyes are dimmer, unfocused, as if just
born, but his voice is deep and clear. The window throbs
in place, the sky a cypher, a structure of belief . . . I see the
folded paper steaming in his fist . . .

WHAT SWAY

What sway in the noncommittal elms or is it the bank of years in which they leaf and fall, window sash, golden hour . . . What if no one came, who looks through the window, who paints the scraggly branches in March, silent as archeology or a ribbon of hair . . . ? And that cool apartment where the swollen elms bled into beveled glass, a local junkie leaning with conviction in the cut shadows of the portico, angular as a March branch in the slant, silent as blood's circuit, silent as dew . . . Who turns, who sways in the orange light, spins like a windblown leaf, *ashes and sparks*, who stretches in the big bay window, breathing-eyes, and steeps a cup of tea, words are swirling, *elm-wood . . . Elmo . . . slippery elm . . .* Who folds the covers back of a book or a bed, and quietly slips inside, and falls awake . . . ?

THE LESSON

He said, "Write about the elements" — or was it the Five
Dimensions . . . or the six Cardinal Dispositions — Was it
dispositions or *positions* . . . and for combat or making love? Did
he *say* that, or simply raise his brow above his fixed eye like a
hypnotist, a mind reader? This I remember: I did everything
I could. This I promised: I'll do everything I can . . . Then
they asked me: Teacher? Then they asked me: Father? Then
they begged me: Daddy! In a wind of time as if . . . In the
seven Grand Spirals and the seventeen Ascending Spins and
the seventy involutions of History in a Bottle: one for the city
on fire, two for the sapling woods, three for the open class-
room with the roof blown off, four for the tour of missile parts
steaming in the ganja fields . . . Five and six for a mix of . . .
How could I respond beyond involuntary gutturals, accidental
rhymes? Write about the ten declensions of salt, he said, or the
fifteen flickers of parakeet blue . . . Write about the twenty-five
rhythms of spring rain . . . So I listened and waited, misremem-
bered or recalled — head bowed in salute to the next word
coming in — So I began . . . So I begin . . .

HE STOOD

He stamped his feet and opened the door, stood on the threshold, turned around. The desert light shrank his eyes, sun slammed his face — he almost lost his breath — blond shiny grasses, ring of distant mountains pinking in the haze, the scorched but somehow fertile earth — he wiped his brow — he couldn't go in, he couldn't move, he couldn't say why — as if he too were a thing dried in sunlight, stopped in his tracks in the heat that fixed him in its gaze — rattlesnake Medusa — where he breathed the stinging dusty winds as though a rock inhaling rock — his proper evolution? — and fed on silence as it flowered and fell — the fierce clarity, the fierce restraint — front door behind him hanging open like a thrown shadow as he blazed in place . . . a man *inside* the view . . . the zooming arc . . . and edge to edge the blue absolute . . .

ONCE . . .

Once I was a sailor in a fiction of the sea for a made-up self on a
boat of text . . . I was happy as a comma when the waves broke,
lifting me like a magic carpet into the changeable mist, then
driving me down through the indigo gulf on a slant of ablu-
tions, erasure. And what of the mist with its long gray hair and
crystal kiss — a little template of the fallen sky, thickened for
disappearing acts — what of its rolling folds, rich as a bisque,
seething like a surname or a lexicon well? And what of the gulf
and its plot-driven plunge, its quicksilver slippages — darting
eels — and leading clues of bluey holes, descending . . . ? Once
I was or could have been or may yet be a magnificent sailor,
spelled out on a graph of azure rills, with hologram eyes that
tell of spillover holds or vanishing dives or shedding selves . . . I
bob in the chop, wail in the spray, plunder the swells . . . And
what of the "was" with its cargo of facts; what of the "once"
with its blown-open hatch . . . and flowering mast . . . and
panoramic sails . . .

TONIGHT

Tonight he is here, surrounded by wreaths of smoke, or *he* is a coil of smoke on the edge of dispersal, or I am a smoke machine and he is mine . . . He is my jelly on the wing — flexing in a mist of muscle, a phantom mass I palpitate and follow . . . Where do we go? The sky is pink. Where will we stay? The blue house hovers; the street a crooked grin of stairs: "What do you want from me, children?" "We want your corners and your closed eyes." I am his rounded side, his safety cave. We take cover in the cool white room, loosed into cool gray shadows — vapor banks — swirl — which are the exhalations of our common lung, our trust exuded and our skin of clouds . . . Where do we stand? Tonight we are here, surrounded by wreaths of smoke . . .

I COULD SEE . . .

I could see calcium going up against the wind, from my desk at my bedroom window as the typewriter clacked like bones . . . "Bones," it wrote, "I sound like bones." I got up to stretch — muscle of my solitude — the typewriter wrote, "The silent orders pull . . ." Was I naked in my grief? — I stroked my beard — the yellow wall stirred — "The yolk breaks," it wrote, "He drips with sweat." Was I clothed in grief, hook and barb; did the yellow room shrink? I cloaked myself in a blanket and circled the room — turn of the screw — threshold and exit — as the crystals form and follow the breeze . . . Clackety-clack wrote, "My black keys are ardor, my red are shame," in a scroll of scarlet ink long as a leg, "Now he busts a rhyme in red . . ." Bones . . . calcium dust . . . shed . . . Are these my mortal shivers? The window shook. I could see the wind rise . . .

THE SHIFTING

The shifting, the silent migration — she fumbled with her lips to find the words — pliable rubies — that fit the hollow of her mouth — but what she intended crossed with what she sounded — a flurry of wings — shifting, silent — blank gasps . . . She'd wanted winter on the corner framing crocus tips in snow; she'd wanted Billy clubs suspended mid-air as demonstrators ran for cover; she wanted what she'd been and seen, a voice-over narration while the park benches filled and emptied like seawater pulsing through gills — and she herself inside the action, swept up or swelled, *talking* as she pulsed, *meaning* as she talked, *finding* as she meant, *giving* as she found, *savoring* as she gave . . . She fumbled with her throat: a grumble, a rolling hiss, some awful whoosh of inner organs . . . and shifted in her chair. If she could mold the air with her fingers and *turn* it like an alchemist, dross to gold — then seize the sculpted words in her fists, and squeeze the meaning out of them! Hunkered down, arms raised, hands whirling, she would close her mouth and eyes and *write.*

TILT

I can see it start to tilt in the rain: the street, the horizon, the cobblestone rise, saturated at the low end, as though the drunken city might catapult its high hills into the flats — with me on their back like a rodeo rider, waving my hat and translating "Yippee ki-ay" into Spanish . . . *"Que te vaya bien,"* they say, "Have a good one." And I do — bucking the cumulus bouncers into the true *azul* that is my matter and my sail. And with you on my back and me on the back of the wind, little friend, we go into the book of the sky as though . . . Oh, crap! The sky's no book, and you're no child, and I'm entrenched in my seat by the window with my ass squirming and my wrong shoes wet! The morning's as long as a morning of rain in a season of thunderclaps over your head . . . "How do you say 'Boom!' in Spanish," I asked, and you said *"Que te vaya bien . . ."* Something gets lost but something is gaining as the big iron bells anneal the *tiempo*, the hour . . . O great Translator in the sky: Be my co-rider, my captain, my thunderhead of rhymes, my catapult at the high end, my little friend, my good one had, my sail, my back, my Boom, my true *azul . . . !*

THE EXCHANGE

Is it a turtleneck? No, it's the calendar. *Is it smeared lipstick?* No it's his pucker of shame. *Are they wilted dahlias?* No they're his stoner eyes . . . [An exchange of value, a tranny shift, a cache of *noms de plume* or *guerre* or *charactère* . . .] *Are they vestiges of youth?* Yes, they are scavenged buds, stoner rhymes. *What are the implements?* The quills of night. *What is their natural habitat?* The vellum of sleep. *Are you sleeping?* Yes I am working . . . [A cognate pool, a feast of semblance, a gift of seeming . . .] *Is it a clean slate?* No it's crammed with erasure. *Are you scribbling?* No I am being scribbled. *What is your* nom de plume *or* guerre *or* charactère? Silvered Tempest or Cauldron Sheen or By the Light of the Full Moo. *Who named you that?* Fate, Chance, and "She did." *Can I go now?* You're already there. *Stoner paradox?* No: street trees in full bloom late summer, gleaming as though wet; cool sun inside a sleeve of ocean air; branches swish in the breeze, lift . . . a high visible hush . . . the *light* light . . . yes/ no, no/yes . . . "I am given to write . . ."

OMIT THE MOUTH

Omit the mouth that answers, like a mindless boner in your face, or a jug-eared boy in the second row waving frantically, "Pick me!" The art is surrender; be stupid and small. In spring I carried my father's limp body to the river's edge where he tried, as ever, to part the shallows. Omit his answer but keep the question: How do you make the river's hair stand up? *I* prefer to watch the trees; their hair I understand though the parts are sere and the bark so long to learn. In summer I loved a willowy boy with a mouth like a hoot owl, an ass like a barn owl, a smile like a horned owl: every part was open at night as he fed on slumber and I surrendered. My mother is a river, *was* a river, the water is old but the form is new. Never presume. Submerge. The water is cold but the form is blue. Your mother is clearer than the shallows in fall and wholly interrogative: The water shimmers and parts; she walks right in. The sport is surrender; omit the question, the worry, the brain, the gender, the judge, the wow, the wonder, the frame, the fret, the ground, the slant, the spin. In winter the snowy owls merged with the field in a gasp of white. Your hair stood up; you staggered, threw out your arms. Omit the circle of stupor, the awe. I cut off my head and walked right in.

THE EDGE

In one variation the stranger sits on the edge of temptation. He has seen and smelled the flower — is already hard . . . In another he sits on the edge of denial; he has eyed the "flower" — and is already hard . . . In a third: he sits on the edge of the bed, toweling himself off — still hard . . . In one variation I am a stranger in a country of hard-edged men, though the air is perfumed with jasmine and the soft clouds could roll you to sleep. In the dream I varied my response from "Yes, I will" to "Yes, I do" to "Yes, I am" to "Absolutely," a perfectly unzipped set of affirmations in the eight cardinal positions of surrender and the nine of imperative power. Every stranger had my name on his lips attached to a different inflection of *"Ay! Papi!"* The rooftop dogs howled inside of every howl we made the dog I am or let them be; the rain of sweat tore the clouds apart that shot the rain from black rolling tanks which tore through our composure as we drank the rain like dogs. In the last variation I've hung my clothes to dry on the balcony edge, like a stranger or a homebody I can't tell, and wring my feet and hands to rid the excess salt, and lick my paw and wag my tail, as I command myself to sit . . .

WE ARE SOME PLACE

We are some place that isn't now, with our bougainvillea shorts in a tangle, and the salt air fresh on our florid lips — but there are no flowers here, no viney pop-ups, no scarlet puff-balls blowing light. We are people who aren't really us, changed by the falling curtains and blocks of ice, the spasms under sheeted clouds of shrieking rain, that pocked our arms with scars like bite marks . . . cinder stars . . . How did we change so fast, dropping our books and wigs in haste, dazed by the silver ripples in the sky that seemed to know our secret wants and needs . . . ? We fell hard, *wanting* to be known, *hurting* to be had . . . as one by one we took the gelatin host, molded into our lungs so every breath we drew was stuck with the gum of who we couldn't be, a thickened gasp of passing phantoms . . . Shaking our heads, arms hacking the air, we fled — but how do you flee the sky? — we stopped — or were we commanded to stop? — we settled — is that the term for falling down? — forever restless in our toes and lobes, heavy to sit and light to think. We are happening sometime that isn't where we are, in a seam of a seal we can't remember or describe . . . and pace the quadrant up and down, and claw the ether as if it were fitted stone, and glance over our shoulders in nervous twists as if we were coming to get ourselves, pale and driven and blazoned with revenge . . .

THE ROOM

"It was like he was in the room" — pushing out the walls — occupying space — belching authority — so I'd be squeezed to the margins in the press of inflation, attenuated like a flagpole and blank as its shadow he saw from the corner of his eyes but wherever I was was the corner . . . How did I win? How did I steal his cup, how did I breathe when he staggered and gasped, how were my feet quicker, tongue sharper, my armor suppler for being annealed to my skin . . . ? How was the sky my ally in which *he* shrank, how was I fast enough to whack his knees with my book, how did I fly when he swallowed all the air in a gulp . . . ? And *she* couldn't help, she hurt, she tried, she bled, she called my name in the wind of receding affection as her voice grew fainter while the wind's roared. Here is my fact: he isn't here. "This was long ago . . ." The room is pink with light, and yellow with light, or violet-tinged with night. I scratch my head and shake my wrists. Of the mark of that thumb on tender skin. Of the forehead burned with shame, the bite of the bridle. Of that endless edict renewable dispossession — as I stumble — *he isn't here* — "it was like he was in the room . . ."

IN THE INTERVAL

To leap and stomp in the dark, to shake the Willis out: in his purple boxers in the hall in the shadow of the streetlight and the rhythm of the rain — not like a dancer, not like a demi-god, not a yogi or a muscle-queen before a mirror — in his flannel shorts with a beach-ball pattern — hypnogogic whorls — in his black socks and no shirt, in his skin and hair and too much sweat in his effort towards levitation in his sack of self, cavorting, to break the frame, the guide-line, the pitcher of decorum, the holding glass, to crack the measure and the beat for the feel of zero or the counter of the wheel in his clumsy turns in his search for grace in the very early morning in the interval extended in his earnest arabesque in his sense of order looping out of place in his changes and his quest for change on his axis in his small house with its pine floor where he leaped and stomped in the dark . . .

SUBMERGED

Submerged deeper than appetite, but *of* the rumbling glands, *of* the steaming juices and their urgent greed . . . She said, "Why did you come," for "Why didn't you come," clutching her abdomen like some pinball Medea, bells, whistles, sirens, spiral eyes. "Let the gristle fly," she said or thought. She had been dutiful to a point, but it dulled the flame in her hair. Who could blame him if he raged in a room without that hair, blue as viscera, empty as the unborn . . . ? In the vacuum load of the endless relative charts — then or now — her or not — "them" or bones isolate — he lost his certainty, swam in loops of appetite or recrimination . . . And the hair, trying to raise its fire from straw, will it burn again . . . ? Will she burn . . . ?

CLEAR

There were plausible echoes of voices, bells, birds, yowling dogs, footsteps, thunder on the move . . . There were hillside houses squared white and flagrant chartreuse cubes, a furor of dark clouds edging the hills . . . I was racing back and forth from the window's formal postcard view to the patio's shameless vista, mapping the violet highs and lows and faraways . . . against my surging immobility . . . I was pacing back and forth from the scratchy mirror in the kitchen to the dimmed-out mirror in the hall, seizing the husk of every disappearing hour . . . against my surging invisibility . . . Unable to read, I squirmed from the slatted rocker to the hardwood bench to crunch up like a sack of sticks and dream of sleep . . . In the thick of the heat I could feel the bones of the nearest clouds smash like boulders, blasting-out a late wind . . . Late churning wind, trashing pigeon's nests, potted plants, and folding chairs; shredding petal, metal, wing and leaf like the End of Days . . . And then this surge and clang of morning light . . . cracks open space . . . stacked up in blazing planes . . . a flare of steps extending . . . as phrases . . . parsed clear . . . from here . . . to where I *see* to be . . .

IN THE LONG GRASS

In the narrow dry tree-tubes — *his* summer in *his* youth — under the pounding sun, and the encasing glare — *his* neighborhood, in *his* pubescent cave — for a retroactive fit of shameless absolution, hot shadow on a cool white page — *my* study in *my* habitat of forms — isometric letters, body rhymes — *my* hidden tower stretching toward zenith but quivering on the rise — in the scratching silhouettes of the dry trees and their pure grief in the dead wind on the stiff flattened grass long stomped gray — *his* story that he told to *me, his* reawakening in *my* waking *him* — of the dry tubes then the wet tubes and the time-lapse and the hunger machine and the indignities eased in his beautiful naked grief in my youth where he grazed in the long grass in the beautiful hot glare like a new blank page open flat in the sun . . .

THE PART UNSEEN

Is this the something else, the part unseen, the antidote of clouds, the sculptural path revealed, the winding staircase tucked behind a maple door . . . ? Is there a person crouching in the foreground, among the rocks and reeds, or jumping in the background — up into the pogo sky with arms akimbo or folded like a chair, daring the bourgeois clouds or *of* them? I think he can't decide whether to fly or die . . . The toreador pants grip his shins — or are those plum trees athwart the Plain of Jars . . . ? Is this his lonesome cataract, the last bushwhack, the foxed and spotted contract, the raison d'être welling up, the parallax . . . ? I think he isn't really there, couldn't see the door, didn't need to cure himself of clouds . . . Is this an alphabet of blood, or disappearing ink? I saw the river peacock-blue mirror from the slowing train in the blue dusk. I think there was a seagull streaking at the bend. It may have been a person in a boat, hauling up his oar to float the curve . . .

MADE A SONG

Floating up and walked along and made a song: "Little Buddha in the clouds, squat upon the rise, what *is* the prize?" And thus, "Oh great woman on the lowland chair — anything is fair . . ." She thought, "Nah, where's the fair in *that*?" and walked some more . . . Woman, Buddha, cloud, chair, floating, walking shadows in the higher air: as I look, screen, worry, dream, work, speak, under your sign of my projection — though high — I bow — to find the particle unseen and bring it home into the sky, my guide . . . So I skip and crawl, puppet of the Mother Air moving puppets in the other air. This is where I dance, where I sit, what I saw and see, as given to me — or look, I can tear up space, tear up the clouds, the Buddha riding on an ozone wheel, free them all, feed them to the book — which always asks for more — tear up the book, feed it to the song, feed *all* to *all* . . . and walk some more . . .

II.

To Make the Air There

CIRCUMFERENCE

What I came for, what I wanted to do, what I thought could be done . . . What was needed, what I was called to do . . . Who called me? Who was measuring change? What was history's name? How did it sound . . . ? Where did I land? Is this the place of rest? Is this a place of action? Did we come together or did I arrive alone . . . ? What I saw in the view, how I parsed the angles and read the stone, how I circled and came back, how I leaned out into the air as if I could smell the news, and squinted to read the scrawling clouds, and grazed my fingertips over the balcony rail to feel the shudder of the wind or the foundation shift, the axis tilt . . . What was the name of the hour I loved, when the water-jug man in the hoop of his rounds sang out the brand of his bottle named for the sky as he climbed the echoing streets, how I stayed in bed in the cool of the call and the heat of your back nestled into my chest . . . What was your name, was it echo or sky? Whose call did you hear? Were you measuring the nights? Did you parse their breathing arcs and read their rise and fall like code . . . ? What was my horizon, how did I know to turn my head? What I said and what I wrote and how I bent and how the light tore through, and how it falls, in widening circles . . . Where I landed . . . What I came for . . . Where I was called . . .

THE FOLD

Then as now — with the light beginning to pale and the waterfront air thinning — then as now, the boy in short pants and gray beard, with a notebook or cool eye or hot heart — and the streetcars passing like scuttling bugs with their cargo of whispering heads . . . Then and now, who made a pool of action where he sat in the still air and the dome of sight in the no-action whispers of an afternoon advancing like a cat . . . It was a moment like a flower in a flower, an inner basket in a basket or an egg inside an egg, whirling in a vortex whose speed resembled silence . . . He licked the folded page. Then as now, a crease within a fold that bent the letters like a bow . . . There's a high window — gull's eye — green glass in a glint of blue — through which he sees, is seen, reviews, is made again or unmade, stripped clear or shaped in planes, unstrung, restrung, where he is mirrored and re-mothered, murdered and slipped back into skin — then as now — while the streetcar slides by in a lull of passing, a pulled stitch in the loose fabric opening like a scroll . . .

AS THE WIND BLOWS

The crowd at the beach, the white sun, the fireworks coming, hum of the copters, my friend said, "The sky cut open," and "The whale breeches, a rider on its back." I listened to them talk — "we" this, "we" that — as though a classroom coughed me up in a dream . . . The small pods of people as the wind blows, the bikes streaking wheel-first in a constant spin down, the run of foliage thick as a ball gown — let them go — the bird formations, the dark armada of hills, the waiting barge, monolithic — let it go — the stomach smooth as porcelain — let me go — I said "mortality" as if it were an appetizer, and "paradise" as though my skin itched. The day was long short slow whizzing by — *magic carpet* — the double knots were tied 200 to the inch, with a sheen that mimicked fire-light off the pile, thick as whale skin yet soft as a sparrow . . . where I lay my head . . . lay my head . . . will · lay · my · head . . .

THE RHYTHM

Once she was a teacher as the wind blows, like a ball gown filling with pink air, she cast a pink dome of shade in which they sat as though it were a room in her mind . . . They spoke in rounds and measured lines as if her silent glances were an invitation to the dance . . . so they danced in patterns and scrawls, over big hungry silences older than snow, they danced *outside* themselves and felt the rhythm of her thought as though the mind itself danced. Once we taught together in a city of winds as the trolleys passed with their skidding feet and gleaming windows pricked by shiny eyes that parsed the city into arcs and bows to form an alphabet of one intent as if the many minds were one mind, one room in which we sat within the hoop of their and our intention as the breeze blows . . . Their patience urged us into speech as though the alphabet had come to life, as though it squirmed and shuddered in our hands as the birds sang in the wind . . . in our living city where they sat in rounds in the pink light of their youth, which we bathed in and borrowed from to tease them into speech . . . as we listened to them listen in the breeze . . .

HERE IS THE DAY

The day was hot/is hot, my skin was hot/is hot, the sticky table hot, the metal pen hot in my hand, the glare metallic off the concrete berm . . . Here is the day, laid out like a plate of noodles: chewy as a novel, thick as July. Somebody mapped the coordinates and just laid it down . . . If I am *in* a chair then I *am* the chair. If I am *on* the street I *am* the street . . . What was I saying? The day has made me, it slit my brain and rearranged the parts that made the day I thought I was, was in. Forgot the broken car window, forgot the money lost: a light bird on the high breeze though there are none, is none . . . If I am *in* the poem then I *am* the poem. Or so I thought or hoped to be, I'll have to see, rewritten or re-phrased . . . The page is hot — I find/I found the day; the day is slit — I meet/I met my way; the way is laid — I eat/I ate the day . . . !

THE OPENING

As if the alphabet first appeared this way, rich with saliva, tucked into the morning breeze as blue receded from the room, the bottles hardened and began to shine, the desk reset its legs and drawers, the carpets bloomed in the hall . . . And not so much to *mean* as to *caress* the elemental things she began to speak their names out loud — the usual sack of men dragged behind her gone with the gone blue, and just this pool of naming at her feet . . . as if some new ark had disgorged her to its plank, and what she called out as she jumped ashore jumped too . . . threw out her arms as though tossing flowers . . . cast a dome of soaring vowels to make herself a home. Like birds sing, she thought, to put structure in the air. Birds sing, she sang, to make the air *there!* — *Bottle, rug, desk, the notebook open like a puff of cloud, the iron bookcase and its precious ribs, the peacock drapes and nacreous window pane* . . . named! — and through the glass *the opening sky, spreading like a fable or a smile* . . . and in the glass her face reflected, smiling as the sleep drained . . . opening into sky . . .

REALMS

You flip through your palette to try to describe the light, fading now in pastel drifts . . . You search for the words to savor the stillness: a ball gown sweeps across the floor without touching; a breeze of silk as the dream flows . . . All of it dream-shine, then? — gown, pastel, summer breeze, birds or no birds in the trees or no trees . . . ? How did the light fall? Widely and lightly. Who trembled in the shift? The skin of the mirror. What was the figure of change? A shuffle of doors. You zip up your hoodie — portable portal — and wait for night to rise like a tent. Then the dark glows and the eyes roll and the book stands as the wind blows like a blank page; you stretch and sort as the ink flows and try to describe the night . . .

REVERIE

Then age with that grabby fist . . . Then age with that dry tongue . . . Then age with its white eyes . . . I was lying on the couch, bucketed in a hollow of the cushions so deep I was almost submerged (then age with its aqueous shoes) in a vision of M, those thick eyelashes fanned-out like a ball gown . . . in a framed Mexican afternoon where no breeze blew but our breaths, drifted up the pink walls and fluttered the curtains by the lemon tree where the birds sang in the no-wind and the birds sing in the no-time . . . then age with its numbered lists, its anyway grin . . . Was it morning or night? — the sofa wouldn't say — fluttering my half-closed eyes — then me with my golden torpor, then me with my somnolent cheer like a boy nursing an all-day sucker or a boy with a sighing puppy in his lap . . . then me in the tidal pull and draw of a low-slung couch, aloft or adrift it wouldn't say as the birds floated by . . .

THE MAJESTIC

She was patient. She watched the walls slide and the floor recede, the windows tremble in the casements and start to warp — (*time passes,* in dependent clauses) — the apples bloomed and swelled up and fell with a thud . . . She had equanimity, she hummed as she held out her fingers like a surveyor and caught the sun in the crook — *medieval* — and sketched a new town raised on planetary transits and the grand arcs of stars, shadows that formed and fell like letters in sequence as the breeze blows — what was a town, a house, a room of sliding walls, a tidal floor that slipped, what was a window *in* or a window *out* and was there a third window . . . ? One strand of cat hair twirled in the air like a propeller — *majestic consequence,* she thought, of one strand, one day . . . She felt proportion — in a tight pony tail and wind-ruffled skirt like the froth of afternoon, with trees for walls, and leaves twittering like sparrows and the breeze as clear as light — *time passes* — or at the big kitchen table — *medieval* — counting the books cracked open on the floor — *majestic consequence* — in her fuzzy slippers where the sun fell on the polished wood like a ball gown spread out in her pink bathrobe in the froth in the oscillating orders of her ever-constant ever-fluctuating house . . .

IN A CORNER CAFE

Everything's implicit in the delicate angle of thumb and fore-finger propping up his chin: pugilist father, mother pietà, Victorian armchair, the ball gown in the closet, the study groups, the long hair, the short hair, the new tattoo looping his ankle, the yoga that leaves him sweating in a heap, the private dance moves — *tour jeté!*, the smart girls who loved him and always hit a wall, the demos and marches, the bicycle that brought him into power, the shorts that met the dare that let the body command . . . Big windows — *holy or mercy* — the diagonal sun swallowing tables as the breeze blows . . . In a corner café — *shadow or sunbeam* — his nose in a book as the letters twitch in the harlequin light . . . *evidence or witness* — and the one who watches, calculates the angle, sucks out the implicit like marrow from a bone — *holy or mercy* — the silvered mirror — the brother . . .

RECONSTRUCTED

This was essential: I had to make the walls sing. I had to tip in the books and tilt them towards memory or suspense; it was crucial; the naked shelves cried as though the new wood were splitting. I had to place the masks so that the eyes burned — who else would stand on guard? — and fit the paintings to the frames, the frames to walls, so image talked to image in all directions as the breeze blows in a storm — I was *in* a storm, *I* was a storm — to make a matrix of spontaneous talk as if the room were blowing bubbles of an alphabet while I circled and spun . . . It was fundamental: I had to bed Lucas, Tony, Mark and what's-his-name (well what's-his-name was standing up) to lubricate the monotheistic air and put blowholes in the ceiling . . . I laid down carpets to animalize the floor — skin and fur — to raise a menagerie of objects and a community of twitching things by which I countered the ever-barking dogs, rolled on my back in the fur of the floor and panted . . . This was vital: I had to learn to walk again, study again, cook again, clean again, cut my hair again, roll a J again, back up my files again, not trip in the ball gown again, hike up my pants, make the bed, shave my neck again . . . to assemble the parts of the day like twigs and spittle for a nest . . . Do you know birds, those flying texts? I watched them through my window, and watched the moon too, and read the phrases of their swoops and orbit-arcs as a book of spells to make the walls sing . . . The walls sang and the masks flamed and the paintings talked and the boys came and the rugs twitched and the spells were set and bad spells broken and the nest wove itself into a cup, a cupped hand, a bed . . . I lay down: It was foundation.

DUET

A bird, a breeze, a tease in time, a rhyme ... A ball gown drifting down, a falling cloud or giant leaf against the sky, a light-balloon and how she watched it soar, like writing in the sky, or like a door of text ... She opened it and fed the dream in time so that the door dreamed no end to time ... I watched her watch, and watching rose like a bird higher than I knew to fly as if I were a cloud of feathers stung by light, and wheeled in loop-de-loops like an alphabet, she thought, a breeze of words teasing out the substance of the sky. I caught her eye in time to see the rhyme as eye to eye we rose, and smiled to be so high and high alike, and rock the light among the feathered words, and fill the sky ...

IN AUGUST

Inner light, outer light, inner war, outer war, his grief, his grief, becomes my grief, his age my age, inner score, outer score, what remains, he said, what's enough, he asked, sun on my back and neck at the table where the buttered rice glistened, sun on the stretched-out cat boneless as a slug, inner light, outer light, late summer in the bleached hills, rolling as if in motion as the cows padded, raised their wet moon eyes when we passed in the hot wind and the hot light, inside and outside, it was, he knew, the moment he asked, and would be, enough . . .

THE MEMORIAL

She lay in the grass under cover of silence, and that many-branched cypress reeking of power . . . where she *wanted* to be squashed, as if interred in the stone slabs inscribed with her name as one of the lost — absorbed into the memorial grove where she lay in the grass. She had seen names she knew; she had known their pain as she could — *below* the grass, *beneath* the tree — in the silence she shared as if memory quieted death in the open air . . . Her cheek to the ground now, feeling the pulse — was it really just hers? — and sensing the underground breath breathing out, always out . . . To be part of the death for a while, she thought, as complicit, as a ring among rings, and a child of the tree, and the scion of grasses, as the witness and warden of no sound . . . here with the undivided, the unbroken . . .

STILL WALKING

Look at the sky: it reeks of projection. Look at my eyes: they're tools of the sky. Look at my feet: still walking. *Which way are you walking?* Ask the birds. *What are you singing?* A walk-along song. *How does it go?* "Bird, dome, pink, breeze ... // mind-light in the alphabet trees ..." And more like that ... Look at my smile: it goes up to the right. Is that my sly inflection, a mark of selection, the pitch of glory, the angle of erection? *All that, but rhymier.* I watched a man who bought a bouquet; pleasure made him wiggle as he walked away. He swished unawares; the peonies winked and smiled to the right. *What was he singing?* A wiggling song. *How did it go?* Back and forth. *Ah, the world's a stage.* Look at the page.

THE THING I WAS

Once or twice I was a sailor, three times, four times, five . . . I said I was or said to be a sailor or a sail or the wind streaking or a sleek hollow hull skimming the rolling waves or the waves . . . What if the wind tore at my back to strip the canvas from the wood, free the oars, cleave the ribs, what if the sea was just a paper view, a fold of sky on a crease of blue . . . ? What if the diagram of stars, the spray, the bounding zeal were what I was told or what I told, pure air, once or twice or ten in the ear and out again, a swinging door . . . and what if the telling stopped, the alphabet unspooled, the leather notebook closed with a snap, done, and, sailor, that was that . . . ? Well, I said, or it was said, once I was a . . . thing . . . moving over a great . . . thing . . . I felt the forward pull of something swift, keen as an arrow, clean as a slice . . . The . . . thing . . . I was slid across the day, skimmed the night . . . and once or again my long hair was flying, flying . . .

ELEGY

What of the sun? It came and went like vanishing ink. I caught the drift, I didn't catch the drift . . . What of the shadows at 4 p.m., incised into the bamboo floor? I read the glyphs, I couldn't remember the glyphs . . . The old poet, where did she go, wrapped in vellum, poised like a caterpillar or bound like a mummy, pulsing with fever but cool as a covenant? I didn't see her disappear, I saw her here. "Come in," she said, *"and taste my meat;"* I read and ate, and read and ate . . . What of The Known? a pebble in my shoe. What of the gown? a diversionary tactic. And what of the sail? a spool of days, a vapor trail, a wing of the sea . . . And the silence? *I reade, and sigh, and wish I were a tree . . .*

SONG

His light, his *light*, from off his face — or was it *in* his face?
Like that shiny planet of the mind that is *in* my sky. He's my
sky for today. *His* light, his *light*, which is *my* light in my mind
. . . Is he *in* my face, are my eyes his sky? He was near translu-
cent after psychedelics when I saw him, was it *my* high, am I
now translucent . . . ? *His* light, his *light,* coming *through* me,
when I saw him on the corner as the breeze blew from the
sky-within or the sky-without like the birds sing in the bird-
trees . . . *My* planet that he made today with his eye- and his
skin- and his sky-light . . . *His* light, his *light . . . !*

III.   *The Inscrutable Edge of Flight*

A MEASURE OF LIGHT

Blazoned with love as a measure of light at the city beach where the wind blows as if on the tongues of the walking men while the spangled water which is my eyes in their glee refreshes the light and the water and the men who are my glee . . . And the families are eating where the shade of the high-leafed maple falls as though sound were muffled of the singing light or the gulls in their hot shrieks who are my tongue as it measures my love and the sun swells in its lowering heat . . . There is summer in the throng in their parti-colored shorts and the orange umbrella and the ambling men with their too-big smiles and too-tight tees as they walk in that way with their hips slung low as though riding the ground that is almost the slither of their low-seated love . . . Wild slow wide day . . . and the herons amassing in a blue cloud with their legs flung behind them in glee which is summer suspended in the long low day as the blue cloud sails . . .

TURNING

Or the colors, I tell you, that the leaves pulled from the sky . . .
As they fell, if they fell, if falling is flying . . . As we gasped, if
we gasped, if gasping is breathing . . . and that gold, we both
thought, or yellow ignited or sun strokes fired of leaves bigger
than our heads — on the corner where they hung from the
trees in drapes as though lit from within, it seemed, or we
were, I guess, by the bright drifts we stomped through and
sailed on if sailing is looking and looking. It was three days
of crimson rebellion and orange confetti on the wing . . .
While the sky beamed to have shot such high glitter from
its great wide smile or I did or you did as we talked as we
walked, if talking is drifting and walking is melting into the
sky's wide smile . . .

THE FORMALIST

It was the same café, the same seat, the same gleaming window, the same light inflaming the new green leaves. It was the same bus rolling by on electric poles, the same alley with the creeping cars. He was the same person with his trembling wallet, the same hungry boy turned senior citizen, holding his pen aloft like a dowsing rod to test the air for rhymes, for the same little notebook with the same insatiable mouth, with his air of benevolent interrogation, and the same resistance to yes-and-no answers in binary form . . . Was it the same afternoon or were they different days . . . ? They were the same marble eyes inside his polished skull, plucked from Greek bronzes at the bottom of the sea, the same seen-it-all sea on the same wheeling planet in the same blown volume of purple space . . . It was the same telescoping phrase in the same expanding digression, and the same moment of amplification at the little square table where he shuffled his butt and squirmed to get position on the chair. While the same menu opened before him like a sky, and he framed for himself hot clouds of steamed milk and soft bread and butter floating by . . .

THE FRAME

If beyond the Scotch pine and such — light in the levitation, light in the eyes — over forest, over hills as though flying — what he sees from where he sits: the frame in which the woods below and such — fog nesting in the far peaks, but he can feel the silver thrill of it — high on the hillside on the far side of — oh — *"life,"* he thinks — If through the frame that holds the door ajar — oh — *"time,"* he says, a stretching pine arced over the valley floor — oh — past time, new time: all the roar of wind at distant edges of the hilltops surround — here in the afternoon (always the afternoon, he thinks) — the convergence — the still point — emptied and filled, chair afloat — into the green — shine . . .

THE PRIVILEGE

Leisure would be sun on this cold day, and time for sun, and a
feel for the sun's arc as a grade of infusion on a graph of spilling
hours . . . So he sat at a table inside a shaft of decelerated time
as a privilege he saw as a bonus — a "retirement package," he
laughed — in a zone of accelerated age for which he seized the
sun as if with both hands, and pulled it close like a lover's body
— a retirement "dividend," he smiled — as if love too had an
actuarial arc and he would use what he could, spend what he
could . . . At lunchtime, with half a sandwich raised in his fist
to punctuate the hour, that he was grateful for, and had lived
for, and would die for, he knew, for lunches too have an arc
— flow through the tunnels of noon thinning to a horizon
itself thinning — and he ducked his head not so much to
avoid the advent as to prepare his aim, without trembling
(the sandwich held still) and with a certain focus as the sun
bled in . . . At the little marble table where he hunched like
a scholar, to sponge up the warmth that swelled the stillness
to fullness and tempered the arc . . . He dusted off the crumbs
like frost, rubbed the gleam on the tabletop as if to polish the
stroke of light . . .

THE VIEW FROM HERE:

SKY ROOM

The view from here includes the view from here — vent of
the maze in amber and rust — and the spill of the bells in
thick waves . . . The view from here includes a man on a sofa,
in a chair, by a railing in the ooze of heat . . . who's pulled off
his socks/my socks — mutant goat — squiggly old-timer —
stands barefoot looking *out* as if looking *in* . . . sails off toward
the bleached hills writhing with anticipation, a thistle for a
boutonnière, and in the pliable haze reels in the daily draft of:
"once when I was *dot dot dot*," or "there where I was *dot dot
dot*," or "how I used to *dot dot dot*" — at a split of the crest-line
as if the dam of memory had its spigot over there — "*mère
des souvenirs . . .*" The view from here resounds with the echo
of Julio's irrepressible purr — *père des souvenirs!* — murmured
in the air, lingered on the breeze — from this pinnacle nest
adventuring out, the rechargeable reach and reel, the memory
garden thick as soup, the fired-up hills in their whispering call,
the oscillating spell, the scope, and this unraveling scrawl . . .

CARTOGRAPHER

Pistons and pulleys — the city's hill-rise and fall — gymnastic — the cobblestone alleyways that map the town, the home, the mind? — finding one's encrypted way without a key — the pink walls, the apricot walls, the burgundy walls — as an enclave of shifting panels, variation shades . . . And he will hoist his belt loop to a pulley in the fierce gymnastic light, and as an *extranjero* — encrypted nation — with his old piston legs slipping and catching — make an enclave in the open air, as public, "in relation" — *camerado*? — with his altitude breath at once tighter and freer — as the city rises and falls like breath itself — projected — as though improvised — variations — that is *his* terrain and *his* mind . . . as he winds the way he has learned to unwind . . . interrogative, unsuspecting, forgiven . . .

SONG AND *DANZÓN*

The view from here's a novelty act, a spectral jam, an overlap: in back of me the scoured hills release the steely mist like top-soil, a peel of gray or shadow grue . . . in front the aerial city lifts its box-tops to the escalating sun, a brimming pool of ore . . . the light . . . in flight . . . The view from here is stitched into my skin as if the hills were mine, the wheeling air mine, the tattered plaza my staging ground and rising stage . . . How I got here: in a dream. Where I came from: a dream. How I walked and how I tore into the bread and licked the glazed pots and stitched my skin into the men who carried me in to the view I made . . . an overlap . . . a fold or two of what I knew and don't yet know . . . a *danzón* in the square with you, you lead, I flow . . . How I thinned and how I grew my hair and climbed the alleyways like a fugitive mule to see the view, and how it changes in the dancing rain, prismatic rush, a thunder wheel, a splattered tear, a train of silver pools and where they flow . . . from here . . .

SPHERE

Here is the view from on high: the planks of bamboo set,
the mossy bridges strung, the squeak of each rung as they
climb, rooftops melting into clouds as they wheel by . . . with
shoulders set, and orbit eyes . . . Here is their view from the rise,
a heap of tinfoil and slate — they stare at the hills as if into each
other's eyes . . . where the jumping spark hides . . . This is their
way, in spectrum altitude . . . a rave of light . . . a falling ray
on low into the empty streets, the cardboard box of day and
vagrant air, the open plaza with its cones of whirling dust,
the iron benches under hanging branches in a precious slip
of shade — this is the jeweled stair they raised . . . from this
outpost with its burnished distant spires that sprang into
view from the wings like a painted screen, a memory play
. . . how they laid the giant blazing strips of sunlight —
almost solid glaze — how they stretched the shadow-spills
and spread their bloom: a looming wedge of laurel trees, a
courtyard arch, a rickety bus-stop hut engulfed by cool gray
folds, the tilted paving stones and mottled earth awash in pools
of sun and shade — this is the living light they made . . . how
they carved up space and flexed the hills into rolling mounds,
and jacked up the streets and pitched the ground — how they
came back to where they began each time and rounded out

the view as if they'd bent the arc, and smeared the sky with
pink, and drank, and bled the ink . . .

Guanajuato, MX

THE PURSUIT

It wasn't a road per se but it was her line of thought, and if she thought too hard she lost her way. Not thinking exactly — more like swimming in air, stroking through medium blue, cloud chambers, crosscurrents, streaks of light . . . Not really swimming but snaking through long grass, tucked under horizon, parting the new blades. If there was shade, she curled up on its pelt; if there was sun she stood in a vertical trance like a tree and dreamed of intent. She wandered "as the new shoots need water," neither for nor against any alternative way, but for alternatives per se. Language seemed to rise in segments like bamboo — footholds in a forward zoom of telescoping phrases she climbed into speech — and she gathered her purposes by coming upon them in pursuit . . . So she walked or swam or thought, on a boundless summer day slow as redemption, following the trail or the groove or the wave. The leaves in the park whirred like feathers, as if the entire hillside were a bird — wing on the wing of the breeze. She leaned into a gust as though it were an idea forming inside her, and for futurity, for discovery per se, surrendered her lead to the wind as the hill fluttered and leaves flew . . .

THE MISSING

He's back at the café where a round marble table is a pool of unfocused thought. He leans, slumping over as if Narcissus nodded off in his own reflection. Where is the love he had before him in his face? Where is the face that called his reflection his name with dewy eyes . . . ? He sits at the bus stop in the spume of late sun — wind spreads light. His brain is dim in the warm flush: How does he come to attention mashed like a boxer, he whose face was articulate in the mirror of a dream as a being in love and light? At dinner encircled by dusk like a plate he eats with his face staring back in the center a ghost medallion — who could he love if not that waning face as a planet unmoored wobbles in space — where is my love he sighs — fallen from grace in a plate — where are my eyes that saw the love in my eyes . . . ?

GO NOW

"Don't wait, don't wait," he said, "Go now." What did I have to lose — a dream, some fabricated scene, a florid map of what I could have been? So I swirled my cape — world on its axis — churn of the cosmic winds — closed around my spinning self as if a new cocoon were spun — and here I am. "Here I am," I said. "I didn't wait, stepped into a little vortex rumbling like a laugh machine . . . and whoosh! Is this the place I meant to be, should have been?" I couldn't see beyond my homely cape of stars, so lay down beneath that stitched-together sky. The dyed blue deepened, unfurled, spread above me, mind-wide — it pricked my painted stars with shots of gold, and licked me with its indigo tongue until my baby blue was true, and sucked me up toward the wilder, unrepentant, high, like a stripped leaf or a slipped sigh . . . above the light, above the line, above the hooking threads and spines, above the spilling ink and guardian files . . . "So *that's* the sky," I thought . . . I tucked in my arms for speed and narrowed my eyes. *"Take me up! Take me up!"* I cried . . .

PROPORTION

What about those trees — cedars — so high — I mean what
if I couldn't, or they weren't, you know, in the park where I'm
so small, to see them streaking up, and all their strategies for
anchoring and sponging sun — where I can be a watcher, so
small in the shade — with their green-chambered hearts and
their high-rising sap and the wind in my ears with my name
on its wrists — so wide — What if that, What if those —
where I slept outside under a canopy of breathing, it seemed
— to be small in the fold while the giant old cedar stretched
and creaked . . .

LOOK

In the early light yes of silver and gray so cool in the heat where you lay on your side as if waiting yes light is made of eyes the bright slash on the bamboo floor where the window sees me watching look at the turreted city so sad and proud in its flash flung out there among the heavy backlit clouds as if yearning power is light privilege is light how stay warm and lit as you curl in the bed like a question mark half open half closed and the morning rushing rushing in . . .

BELIEVER

He wanted to wander; he wanted to get lost; he wanted to fuck up and get found; he wanted to fly backwards — on a broomstick in reverse — until the cooked and the raw came together . . . *under the jacaranda* she would say as if it were a myth of sound . . . He made up a place a town a day in sunlight and went there; the mountain was real as it looked down on him inventing himself in the gleam. *Madrugada* she'd say as if they were bathing in a river . . . For sure he watched the buildings fill in the heat, infused with pastel blues and pinks deepening by the hour, till noon overflowed its banks — and then the thick, extracted, steaming sheen laid down to seal the houses in their painted skins . . . Yes, someone speaks to make a person in the blank space of the vista where the sky melts. Who listens, watches, springs — like a bird veering south — "a light in sound, a sound-like power in light" high in the stream — for the pure angle of inception, the inscrutable edge of flight — believer — and the company of wings . . .

THE SPIN

Once I was or said I was or it was said a sailor. The bounding main, the winds of change, the pulsing tides, the weight of wood, the telepathic mast and bending sails, the blessed implacable stars, the brine in my hair and mouth and eyes: *my* story, *my* time . . . Oh, once I lied or was a lie, a land-locked lub with a fear of the sea who never met a prow or jib, an anchor or an oar, a wave of blue or a wave of green, a rudder or a plank . . . Another lie! I never knew the land at all, or air or ocean, crystal shallows or shadowy deep. I said the words I read them in a book, the book I was or read myself to be. And made the sails that split the spine and fled the page and hoisted up the sign that said I was and read I was a sailor . . . So then, it had to be, it was, I was a sailor, my famous wild and curly hair a sail itself, and you my undertow and tide, my roaring wind and keel, my climbing wave, my farther shore, my rim of stars: my *Reader* . . .

ON THE STEPS

How we linger on the steps at sunset; the traffic slows — red brake lights flare in the dusk. We watch as the people disgorged from the buses walk by walk by — all business from business to home. How we linger who live here as the walkers walk faster to be where we already are where we're watching unseen on our stoops — covered already by folds of dusk breathed from our homes as we linger so lucky with brains smoothed and muscles unstrung to be already here where we are. How the clouds pink-up as the cool air settles and the hot metal dulls on the cars so many that move slower than the walkers who lengthen their strides and quicken their paces to be where they'll be. It's as if our backs were warmed by the fire as we sit at the mouth of a cave on the stoop with our foyers and lobbies and vestibules open behind us already lit and we turn to re-enter the arms of our silencing dens like sleepwalkers hushed and already enveloped in part by the evening descending on the stairs and the steps and the stoop of our homes . . .

AIR AND SKY

Air and sky — *So what else is new?* — The sky in his pocket, a lift in his step — *The same sky?* — But a different pocket — *How does it fit?* — He breathes like a cloud — *What of the rain?* — If only — *What of the rain?* — We call it sweat — *What of the rain?* — It pools in his shoes — *What kind of man is he?* — An aeronaut — *What's his allegiance?* — His allegiance is to the horizon — *What direction is that?* — Through the hole in his pocket — *A hole in blue* — I just met a man with indigo eyes and a cumulonimbus smile — *What does that mean?* — It means he rained smiles — *Again with the rain?* — El Niño — *What was his name?* — Catch Me If You Can — *Did you?* — Look in my eyes — *The world is vast* — Put your hand in my pocket — *Oh my!* — Of course I caught him — *I know, I saw your iris pucker and throb* — Eyes read other eyes — *Sky writing* — The blue rises — *How does it feel?* — Like space, like mind, like breath, like light, like free-fall and spinning and floating and rolling and hovering and looking and reading while sleeping and kissing with your eyes closed and dancing in twilight — *Air and sky?* — And so I fly!

IV.   *Shiver*

SHIVER

for San Francisco

I.

GREEN EYES

Now what I saw was the same but my eyes were different, turned green like my mother's immediately after she died. How did she die? Incrementally. Long gone now ago in some space, historical, as though stretched thinner towards air . . .

And me too pulled into threads, or you in your smoke drift who have come so far to read the clouds and stars in their formation on a page . . . He remembers corn dogs and bulldogs, dreamsicles and ventricles, leather belts that whistled

and struck, and cabbage soup to soothe the hiss and the strike. Not in sequence but stacked like plates and conflated . . . And those pinwheel clocks spinning forward *and* back. A boy is a prelude, then an afterthought, then a molten core . . .

He armed himself with elocution and adorned himself with pride. Like a thief in plain sight he stole gender from the fembots and dude-droids, layered his body with faux leather and faux lace, muslin printed with snake sigils,

and saris of indigo denim fit for a wrangler — one with ban-
gles big as cow eyes, that is, lighthouse beams that swept in
widening arcs as he twirled, to flame the countryside like a
dragon, set the village ablaze as the dragon in drag

he was, on fire, or so the cops thought when they stopped him
for flying without a leash and buried his head in their waist-
handy hood, by which I retired into the ground with a groan
of lavender fumes, which will henceforth be my subtitle

when they exhume me in my marble book. Yes I talk as if I
lived, but the fiction of me is merely your pleasure in decon-
structing the violent world, so I dance with arms akimbo in an
interrogative stance, and sing out of tune

as I do for a music of bent aspirations and uncommon grace.
You remember that drinking fountain you led him to, and
tipped his face into the black water so he could taste the poi-
son syrup in its full splendor, fragrant as burning shame,

with a nose of infallible encyclicals and notes of medieval
edicts tacked to stone walls? Yes, he carried that spice to make
the man inside him thirsty for good, un-slaked, with a tongue
for negative capability and lips formed to

suck the juice from the bones he raised. Where did the sky come in? When did it sever the present from the past and eat the human terms, the diminutives and endearments? How did the blue start to glow in our hands and

bloom in our faces as we shed our scales, how did the new skin bristle like parchment as we spoke to each other in welts and rashes the new text of the new alphabet of the new history . . . ? If I say "the past" I mean my mother.

If I say "my mother" I mean the boy I was. If I say "I was" I mean something was here condensed from the air with a specific gravity you hung a name on — if that was you hanging names under the eucalyptus leaves in the rain.

I hang on your every word as the city shivers, words like "mortgage," my beloved, and "high-rise," my evil twin. The city shivers. The city shivers. Now what I saw was not the same but my green eyes . . . my mother shivers . . .

my green eyes . . . He remembers how you tasted bathed in his sweat, he remembers how you tasted roasted in his juices, your nipples spurting and your hips flexed on his incline, how could he not remember, an ocean more, more wet, more rushing, more swells, more salt, of that contribution the verses are written in shivers . . . my green eyes . . . remember . . . And the story about two men in kilts or culottes, the story of two women in jackboots and capes, of four men

and six men and ten men who shivered in silver streetlight in contraband rain in communal moonlight till morning shot the city with frost or glitter now the city doesn't shiver . . . The city doesn't shiver. In Part II I discover the cure

for allegiance. In Part Seven I dismantle the binary system as a scam of chiaroscuro for the rainbow impaired. He drank his coffee — elixir of measure — at the sidewalk café, dodging belt-bombs and snipers defending their tables

or standing on chairs in an ambush of lectures on right thinking, right acting, right killing, right versing and if in the end he was beheaded for forgery or failing to inspire his green eyes no longer remember . . . but time slowed

as my mother receded into that space where vectors converging unravel like a knot in my heart loosened or hers under surgeon's thread pulsing free, an explosion of sorts, and flowed onward . . . The city shivers. That was my home you sold, my golden nest, my chamber of solace, my secret place of rest, that was my chair for age and my couch for sleep and my desk for sleeplessness and my rug for bedazzlement, that was my work you sold that framed

the walls as if they lived like eyes, green as the lunging trees outside, the city the city the city shivers. Do you remember that hilltop above the hilltops where light fell like water to drench our wide-open faces and the whole thing

spread out before us coast to Bay, rise and fall, as we locked hands to seize and store the image and our lingering kiss drew in the streets and parks and timbered houses and raw incendiary sky as if kissing were breathing,

still breathing, pressed together as one inhalation, the city inside us, rise and fall . . . my mother breathes . . . her green eyes . . . open wide, my same eyes . . . open wide. The city . . . shivers, its green eyes . . . breathe . . .

II.

HOUSE OF AIR

How does time with its hammer and tongs . . . so that invisible
. . . the past invisible . . . *House of Air*, he said . . . He was climb-
ing a wooded trail, which may have been a dream or a vision,
as if climbing itself were an ark to the visible,

and the red, slick madrones, the twisty manzanita shrubs,
clawed through the time or the fog or the curtain of air and
refused to back down — surveyors or sentinels — inviolable —
rooted in the rank . . .

Would you bring me back if you could, would you strip the
mausoleum to see my happy face again, with its echoing
eye-sockets and omni-grinning jaw, would you dust me off,
blow out my nostrils, fit me with lips of pearl

to revisit our nacreous kisses, slick as oysters and silver-blue as
their shells . . . ? invisible kisses . . . How does time with its
hockey stick, its crack of polished wood . . . ? Would you call
me back to feed on your prime . . . ?

She is back at her desk, that sifting machine . . . She is caught
framed in the window by a passing gull. She sees what she
sees, though what proof is that? Against the wall of books —
shelves of Honduras pine — her silhouette flayed

by the blinds, she lists in sequence the towns burned, the cities under water, what she remembers and what she's been told, what she's read in The Book of Slaughter and The Book of Stains, The Codex of Compton,

and the Index of Vanishing Holes, her sifting machine chuffing like an engine as her hand moves like a wand . . . invisible grief . . . in the House of Air . . . on a Thursday afternoon . . . as though living inside a ravenous scroll

that lengthens as she reads, of which she is the author or the scribe she can't tell, and runs her fingers through her hair to slow down the march of time so she can breathe . . . she breathes . . . and time slows . . . and time slows . . .

Once I was a sailor when the sky was one thing, a blue breath from pole to pole I caught in my wild hair and out-flung hands as if *I* were the boat I sailed, and streamed on the gleam off the waves to any place I named . . .

Once under the unified sky that blew itself in gusts of blue that filled his mouth with air that took the shape of names he shouted, and banked into the wild verses that claimed the places he needed to be or go — invisible vision —

by which he traveled to himself and back in a blue cocoon of voices as if he were the sail, the boat, the sky, the wind, the mounting waves and rushing air, the place he wanted to see, the person he wanted to be, he was, once, when, a sailor.

Take her hand as she parts her hair and wipes her brow. Is it a butterfly of thought? Remember what she can't forget. The children with their eyes like dinner plates, the wiggling dog, the imprint on the mattress

and its shape of smells — invisible ardor — How does time with its shovel, its iron clang . . . ? She adds your name to the list. She won't forget you, visitor, denizen, prisoner, supplicant, émigré, traveler, stopping by this house of air . . .

III.

BREATHE

My green eyes floating in the dark . . . And breathed as if the
sky were sitting on my lungs. It has to be communal. It has to
be beyond remembering or forgetting. The pages need to rustle
and turn by themselves,

as if the wind of the arriving news were blowing from start to
finish, front to back . . . invisible book . . . My mother reads,
her green eyes peel back the letters . . . And then he just seemed
to come apart in his limbs,

like a marionette with strings snipped — and would've fallen
to the ground were he not already scraping the ground — his
eyes with their retinas lifting away in shock — and the floaters
zooming in like drones of the vitreous . . .

Invisible vision . . . now, yes, but behind the steel mounds, the
hubs of digital clouds or digital air or electric packets deliver-
ing shivering sums of shivering sums, the city denuded, the
hills leveled and the valleys filled in . . .

He sold his pillow for $5k . . . It has to be collective, it has to be
grabbed by the throat and shaken . . . or was that you shaking
me out of slumber, as I woke to clouds of plaster dust circling
the room like a tiger, the bricks and timber

shattered in the cold . . . the city shivering . . . Which was the real history? Was there more than one? One behind another behind another . . . Who arrived, who left, who stayed against all odds . . . ? Who danced on the tabletops

in a flurry of pastel scarves and three-day stubble squealing, *"spacioussssss,"* and built a theatre out of Kleenex boxes and nail polish for a musical version of *Long Day's Journey into Night* — in Pig Latin! — and brought the house down;

or sailed away on the barques of the epidemic from Laredo to ruin with a smile that wouldn't fade and a free pass to a convo with the angels; or got priced out, evicted, and laid off all at once but was saved by her business

of hand-made organic shrouds, no irony . . . one behind another, not in sequence but stacked like plates and conflated. If I say "I remember," does that mean I made it up? If I say "made it up" was history my evil twin? If I say "history"

I mean I dreamed something sifted and resifted stayed in the bottom of the pan . . . It has to be cooperative like the wind and the sail . . . As if time with its telescope or microscope she couldn't tell . . . slowed in the distance and slowed in the foreground and her hand slowed too as the list lengthened . . . I remember . . . I made it up . . . invisible images . . . Everyone breathe . . . Once, in the early years, he married the city, on a jagged outcrop on top of a hill

with his eyes clear and the air clear and that blue-jewel horizon and his pledge of intent with his heart clear in his deep-breathing chest I take you, he said, and that clarity, that northern light, which made everything visible all at once,

with no clouds no smog no shiver no shock every cornice and balustrade, every cedar and pine, every dizzying hill and dune and tower and scalloped beach at the western edge, with the green eyes of my mother, the painter,

growing into mine, and time wide open as though stopped or unending — I do — and the covenant like a poem wide open and unending . . . invisible innocence . . . and the joy of the wind . . . Everyone breathe . . . The city

behind the city . . . You were there, I remember, with your velvet tunic embroidered with leaves (I coveted) and your straw hair in a ponytail and a gentle smile on half your face while the other half courted a lascivious leer,

and both touched me in my hard place . . . the city shivers . . .
I think we walked all day and talked nonstop for hours till
midnight stopped our chatter and my bed swallowed us like a
lotus closing and did we wake?

Did that bed ever disgorge us? History is a vision of a version.
It has to be a collaboration, it has to be stopped and started in
the joy of the wind. My mother shivers . . . She remembers the
fierce clarity of light . . . It shows

what it needed to show, so she paints what she needs to see. I
saw you from a distance: scriptural, and from close up: devo-
tional, and from inside: sacramental. I may have made you up
out of necessity. That was my home

they sold . . . Everything shivers . . . he said, "I do . . ." The
sky can tell the difference between what's in front and what's
behind . . . My green eyes . . . Still kissing in the blue blue light
. . . One behind another . . . Everyone breathe . . .

IV.

FLIGHT

Is it an elegy? Was it made up in a sigh of the wind? She checks her barometer as the scroll flaps like a flag . . . She writes as if in a trance, twisted by the torque of plate stacked over plate: a litany of migrations, displacements,

evictions, and lockouts, of monoliths tilting, and falling block-ades of shade . . . her boxes full of flattened faces and the string of names rising like smoke. They inspected the floor, the foun-dation, the walls, the sheetrock

and bedrock, the doorjamb, the beams, but the fissure was in the vision . . . invisible vision . . . My green eyes burn. I remem-ber the joy of the torque of the wind, with my hair flying and my blue tunic in full wingspan

and my arms locked in numberless interlocked arms and the streets slick with dew at any hour . . . Everyone breathing . . . Was paradise my evil twin? Did it tar the future with the past — invisible shadow — and draw down the lumbering sky? Now yes, but the sky behind the sky! I remember . . . We made it up . . . He looks around him in a stupor in the corner of his small room on the bentwood chair he clings to in perpetual quake . . .

shivering in the temblor of rent-times-twelve . . . and calculates the holes that will land him in her Book of Voids — as she follows her own shivering hand, alive like a slithering cat stalking the last page. When he remembers,

his eyes begin to clear, her hand pauses mid-phrase. If he remembers, the sky jacks up. Is forgetting my evil twin? If I say "him," does history let me in? One after another as my mother watches from her hospital bed

still smiling in full sail as she breathes forward and the future forms in her green eyes . . . It has to be weathered arm in arm. It has to be made-up and put into action and released into the wild. The city shivers in my twitching eyes.

Is it anticipation or regret? I think we never got out of bed, never should, never will, and the warmth remains. I think the scent of common purpose lingers like a map of silver dew. One summer day under full sail he stood high up on a cliff top at Land's End — ocean's edge — where the pelicans in their pterodactyl way formed themselves out of the visible distance in a forward line, and flew right by him eye level . . . face to face — their leathery grit

and bony grace . . . and kept coming single file as if made up by the sky — emissaries or remnants — with their ancient topaz eyes set for primordial crossings . . . alert to his but fixed further in common purpose . . .

and the green eyes of the great golden bridge watching . . . and the thrill of the wind . . . one by one behind another they flew so close to my high-cliff perch I seemed to fly with them, into their visible distance with the old city

high inside me as though breathing me into the future in my own now-prehistoric skin and bright purposes — I do — and the pelicans making me up in perpetual migration on a forward wing . . . invisible horizon . . .

and time slowed or the sky slowed or the wind went still and the cities merged as my mother's eyes saw what they needed to see . . . the city *in* the city . . . still kissing in blue light . . . He settles his breath to steady his hand, sings a song he thought was a dirge but may be a lullaby for the newborn — take my hand or wing — It has to be locked arm in arm, flung in formation out of the hole in sky . . . The city quivers . . . It has to be made . . . It has to be made . . .

V.

SHAKE

A shiver is a rip in time. He puts his ear to the ground where the deep magma sings. History is a version of the future, a sweep of pterodactyl wings in rising light . . . The pavement quivers like jelly but doesn't split as the hot steam

vents . . . The future is underground: the city *beneath* the city. It has to be endured while the crippled buildings sway, molded when still hot, sculpted in the thrill of the wind . . . She watches from a distance, waiting for the ink to dry,

hand raised high in the air as if trying to escape the pull of the page . . . She wants a new sheet clear as an alien sky, blue-white and tight right to the edges. And Boom! It was like someone had dropped a piano on the floor above me —

more a thud than a shake — except I lived on the top floor, no one above. Then a groan as though something trapped below wanted to get out/get in . . . The house shivered and shook. If I say "open" is hot lava my evil twin?

With his night-vision goggles — green eyes — he looks for every crack in time, every seam about to slip, every hollow and hole — to let the old city roar in and wake the sleeping walk-ing un-looking pixel-bound dead . . .

Where is the sky now? Does it pulse like an organism, does it breathe in silver waves and tremble like morning dew? The sky beneath the sky! And you with your long hair like strands of fire — I think we burned up that bed —

I think we live in those flames, still burn — I think our kisses are comets in the shivering sky . . . And in the hot silence of the blank streets he walks as if in a trance, with time stretched and stacked like plates, and my mother's eyes

squinting to keep the plates conflated — invisible gravity — while the temblors rock his footsteps and the wooden houses squeal in their beautiful joints and the violins of the tall cedars wail their ache and awe . . . up the steep hill

behind his house where the downtown towers seem already pitched forward, ready to fall, and the far-out Pacific racing in — green eyes of the deep water where the bones of the buildings lay . . . the city quivers . . . now, but before

the great shiver . . . He buries his face in his cupped hands as if submerged in deep water, holding his breath to stop time and lock in the memories — her raised arm aching but desperate to live the pause, to hold back the footnotes on tent cities, tossed syringes, immune deficiencies — and release the city from its litany of litanies . . . He spins in place to keep his balance and ride out the shake — history is a whirlpool from which only the spinners wake —

in common purpose out of a hole in the sea — I remember — hot lava made me . . . What did they see? What did they know? How did they work? How did they work together? Who did they want to be? Who did they become?

How many had green eyes? How many loved history? Whose mother's heart blew apart its sutures in a last attempt to keep the ways in play . . . ? Once I fell to the floor in my little house in a skylight beam of almost solid sun

and lay my cheek on the bamboo planks in a pose of surrender and a shiver of thanks . . . Once we climbed the distant mountain in the eastern county after big rain with the thick mud congealing around our shoes like bear traps,

locking our steps . . . Still we trudged on, mud-bound, not for the summit per se but just to see from the top the city across the bay shining in its sheath of western light, with the glamorous fog like a sequined cape on its shoulders jeweling the shadows — "sunset couturier" — and the red-tinted hawks wheeling in a vortex of suspended breathing . . . the city shimmers . . . Once in a park in a cool breeze with my notebook un-sutured in my lap

I watched the hummingbirds in their mating dance climb the air out of sight then plummet straight down on an axis of love in flight — flickers of red and green in a daredevil swerve of light . . . Once I met a man in a bar . . . Once I met a man

at a café . . . Once I met a man in the drugstore up and down the shadowy aisles . . . Once I met a man and once I met a man . . . I do . . . and rode the wind in my sheets to make our bodies shiver on an axis of love in flight . . . I remember

like it was tomorrow . . . Which city through the tumbling night? Long long ago he would ride the late late bus into the city with his eyes not yet green but pressed like suckers to the window glass to see the spires lit up as if on fire

with his heart lit up as if on fire and the hot lava of his blood . . . and he seemed to pitch and stagger through the late streets on the quaking jolts of the city under the city — tossed around in the torque of desire that would unmake him and make the city his — indivisible citizen — arm in arm hand in hand — I do — How we take the brilliant northern light and . . . how we face the monstrous towers in their sky of shade to . . . how you grab my hand so we can . . .

how we inhale together on a silver wave of . . . how our notebooks tremble with their diagrams of . . . how he bends to kiss his mother's forehead just to . . . how his green eyes slice through traffic, mammoth buses, lonely shopping carts so . . .

how she lays down her pen and closes the book and walks out the door for . . . how we gather in the plaza and thread each other's eyes on a pledge of intent to . . . how we tack a notice to the door for . . . how we close our eyes to dream

and open our eyes to dream . . . on the lip of the western edge . . . How I bear down into the stacked worlds where my now-green eyes gleam, and parse the realms and track the turns and scan the prepositions — *behind, in, under* —

to meet the city that made me and that I make — by wing or by shoulder, on an axis of love in flight — one behind another inside another beneath another . . . with the sky pulsing, molten . . . and the city breathing in the blue blue light . . .

ACKNOWLEDGMENTS

Grateful acknowledgment is given to the editors of the following publications, in which some of these poems first appeared:

Amerarcana, Berkeley Poetry Review, comma, Elderly, Fourteen Hills, High Noon, Lavender Review, New American Writing, Recours au Poème [France], The Zahir Review, Volt, Your Impossible Voice, A Dusie Sampler, The PIP anthology of World Poetry of the 21st Century volume 10, The Portable Boog Reader 8: Part II, the Duration Press chapbook *Reverie: A Requiem*, online for the Academy of American Poets at Poets.org., and in the book *Flowers & Sky: Two Talks*.

Gratitude, too, to the many friends who read (or listened to) part or all of this work as it developed, and to Nightboat's indomitable Kazim Ali and Stephen Motika, for indomitability.

"He Stood," "The Part Unseen," "Song," and "Still Walking" originally published in *Flowers & Sky: Two Talks,* Entre Rios Books, 2017; reprinted by permission.

AARON SHURIN is the author of fourteen books of poetry and prose, most recently *Flowers & Sky: Two Talks* (2017), *The Skin of Meaning: Collected Literary Essays and Talks* (2015), *Citizen* (2012) and *King of Shadows* (2008). His work has appeared in over forty national and international anthologies, from *The Norton Anthology of Postmodern American Poetry* to Italy's *Nuova Poesia Americana: San Francisco*, and has been supported by grants from The National Endowment for the Arts, The California Arts Council, The San Francisco Arts Commission, and the Gerbode Foundation. A pioneer in both LGBTQ studies and innovative verse, Shurin was a member of the original Good Gay Poets collective in Boston, and later the first graduate of the storied Poetics Program at New College of California. He has written numerous critical essays about poetic theory and compositional practice, as well as personal narratives on sexual identity, gender fluidity, and the AIDS epidemic. A longtime educator, he's the former director and currently Professor Emeritus for the MFA Writing Program at the University of San Francisco.

NIGHTBOAT BOOKS

Nightboat Books, a nonprofit organization, seeks to develop audiences for writers whose work resists convention and transcends boundaries. We publish books rich with poignancy, intelligence, and risk. Please visit nightboat.org to learn about our titles and how you can support our future publications.

The following individuals have supported the publication of this book. We thank them for their generosity and commitment to the mission of Nightboat Books:

Kazim Ali
Anonymous
Jean C. Ballantyne
Photios Giovanis
Amanda Greenberger
Anne Marie Macari
Elizabeth Motika
Benjamin Taylor
Jerrie Whitfield & Richard Motika

This book was made possible by a grant from the Topanga Fund, which is dedicated to promoting the arts and literature of California. In addition, this book has made possible, in part, by grants from the National Endowment for the Arts and the New York State Council on the Arts Literature Program.